DEAD MAN
WALKING

How I Went From Convict and Drug Addict to CEO and International Speaker

The True Life Story of

ORLANDO SALINAS

For permission requests, bulk sales, booking for speaking engagements, etc., write to the author or publisher at the address below.

Choose to Change Foundation
2112 W. University Dr. #608
Edinburg, TX 78539
Phone: (956) 929-9560
www.Osalinas.com
www.Choosetochangefoundation.com

Unless otherwise stated, scripture quotations are from the King James Version (KJV).

ISBN: 978-1-7201-5332-0 (paperback)
ISBN: 978-0-463-56034-1 (eBook)

Printed in the United States of America

I dedicate this book to:

My precious wife, Isabel. I say thank you so much for your faith and also choosing to believe in the impossible for our lives.

To my mom I say thank you for your love and the amazing example of motherhood you have always shown our family.

And to my daughter Karen Beth I say: I have dedicated my life to helping men become the fathers, husbands and leaders they are supposed to be in hopes that I can help more children to never have to go through what you had to endure, *fatherlessness.*

TABLE OF CONTENTS

INTRODUCTION

January 17, 1997, Ten p.m. Saturday Evening.

I am sitting on the living room sofa watching TV. My wife and I were living at my mother's house because we had nowhere else to go. The only reason we were there was because my mother felt sorry for my wife, Isabel. My mother knew she was having to raise her two daughters and that I was just a loser drug addict. I'm thinking to myself, "Where can I get another hit." It was now ten p.m. My wife comes out of the bedroom and says, "Orlando, please watch the kids. I am going to take a shower. Please don't leave."

As soon as she gets in the shower I go into the bedroom and search for her purse. I found it in the closet along with some kids' toys she had also hidden. I took her last twenty dollars and I left. My wife was going to use these twenty dollars for our daughter Andrea's fourth birthday the following day (Sunday, January 18th).

I left walking because I didn't even have a vehicle any more. Not even a bike. I had pawned everything I had. I was a loser.

1

I got to my drug dealer's house at twelve midnight. There was no one home. So I sat there like an idiot until four a.m. when my drug dealer pulled up. He knew me well. He knew what I wanted. I was one of his favorite customers. He got out of the car and just threw the twenty dollar little bag of cocaine at me. I went to the back room, where I usually went, and fixed up my syringe. It was dark so I wasn't able to see very well. I put it in my arm and bam, slammed it all in. I couldn't believe what had just happened. I didn't get high! I had missed. I had missed the vein. And for a drug addict like me that is like the end of the world. I was furious! Something very wicked happened to me at that very moment. I said to myself, **"I am going to get another hit and I don't care who I have to kill!!!!"**

I made up my mind that I was going to go rob a store and I knew exactly which one. The 7-11 on the west side of town. So I walked across town and got to the 7-11 close to six a.m. Now Sunday morning was my daughter's fourth birthday.

It was almost six a.m. and I am standing in front of that 7-11. I've been out all night long. I am debating if I should go in and rob the store or just go back home. "Do I rob the store and risk going to prison for the rest of my life or do I just go home?" The clock says five-fifty-eight. "In two minutes," I said to myself, "I'm going to go in at exactly six a.m." My heart and mind are racing. I am thinking of all the things I've done in my life. All the messed up things I have done. The stealing, the cheating, the lying, and manipulating. The people I've hurt, the pain I have caused my family and friends. How did I ever get myself in this mess! How did I become such a hard-core loser drug addict? I just wanted to die!

I didn't care anymore. In my mind I knew this was exactly what sin does. It destroys not only your life but it destroys the lives of the people around you. The people you say you love the most. It's amazing how the devil works. Destroys your very soul. I was just a dead man walking. I just wanted to die! The truth was that I had died a long time ago. I'd been putting needles in my arm for ten years now. Just a few hours earlier I had stolen my wife's last twenty dollars. She was going to use that money today for my daughter's fourth birthday. I was just a loser drug addict!! I was worthless — a loser father, a loser husband, and a loser son! I was hopeless!

The clock turned to six a.m. I made my decision. I ran into the store and put my hand in my pocket and pretended like I had a gun. I yelled at the clerk, "Give me the money! Give me the money!" The cashier gave me sixty dollars and I grabbed the money and ran out the door. I was going to my drug dealer's house. I knew what I had just done. If I got caught I was going to prison for the rest of my life. I was going to go get sixty dollars worth of cocaine and just shoot it all up. I just wanted to kill my worthless self. But I didn't make it too far. Before I even got halfway, Edinburg PD had surrounded me. But I kept running and they ran after me. They threw the black stick at me and down I went. It was over. I was done! I was going to go to prison for the rest of my life and I knew it.

This is where I found myself at the age of thirty-three, January 18th, 1997, on my daughter's fourth birthday. I was hopeless.

CHAPTER 1
My Father

My father came to America at the age of six with an older cousin that was fifteen. Six years old — can you imagine? He started working in the fields with his cousin and the Salinas family finally took him in and adopted him. He didn't want to go to school so he only went to the third grade. In other words my father started his working career at six years of age. Wow!!

My mother was a very loving and caring woman. She always took us to Catholic mass and did her best to help us in every way she could. I know today that my mother was an angel sent from heaven just for me. What a privilege it is to have a mother like mine. For the record I would like to take this time to say this: "Everything I am and everything I hope to be, I owe to my mother."

I was born in Joliet, Illinois. I have two brothers and two sisters, Pete, Adrian, Lydia and Diana. When I was five years old my parents moved my family and me down to South Texas, to a little town called Hargill in the Rio Grande Valley (The RGV).

5

This is a region of South Texas on the border of Mexico. It is called the RGV because of the river that separates Mexico and Texas, the Rio Grande River. The RGV is made up of five counties and over one hundred plus small towns and cities, with a population of about 1.5 million people and rapidly growing. I call the RGV the best kept secret in the US. The bigger cities in this region would be cities like Brownsville, Harlingen, Edinburg, McAllen, Mission and Rio Grande City.

I lived in this little town of Hargill, Texas, from the age of five to fifteen years old. I actually have good memories of my childhood. If you ask my parents they would probably tell you I was a good kid. But they would probably be the only ones to say that. From what I am told I was just a high energy kid with a very adventurous spirit. In today's world I would have probably been diagnosed with all kinds of disorders and been put on some sort of medication. My memories are like scenes of a movie or just selected moments in time. Fishing, riding my pony, climbing trees, swimming at the lake.

I had one brother and two sisters. My brother Pete had gone into the Navy, My two sisters, Diana and Lydia, were in their own little world. I remember having a pony my dad had bought for me. I was always riding my pony back and forth on the dirt roads in this little town we lived in. My uncle Benjamin would call me the "pony express." I remember always being outdoors. I would play in the woods, make slingshots, and shoot my BB gun. My best friends were

Franky and Bobby, my cousins. I actually had several friends now that I think about it. Let's see, there were Rene and Romeo, Eddie, Willie, Ruben, Baldo, Rene, Bobby, the Cardona brothers and many more.

I just remember being carefree and full of life. I was an explorer, a dreamer. We would play football together and play with little cars in the dirt. I remember one time playing tackle football on a dirt road and I fell and broke my collarbone. That ended my football playing career at the age of twelve.

I grew up knowing my parents loved me. They were hard-working people. My mother worked in the sewing factory for Levi's and Haggar's and my dad worked as a cook at a restaurant. I remember my mother waking us up every morning for school. She would leave us pancakes and eggs ready-to-eat as she would rush off to work.

I remember running home from school every day so I could catch my favorite shows, *Batman* and *The Six Million Dollar Man*. I thought they were the most awesome shows in the world. Then when I passed to eighth grade I now had to catch the bus at seven in the morning along with my brother and sisters.

My father was a hard worker. I never saw much of him but I knew he cared for us and loved us. My father was a very good provider. I don't remember ever lacking for anything. I now know we were poor but I didn't know that back then. We even had an out-house (A bathroom outside).

I never really considered my father an alcoholic but drinking was his thing. BBQ on weekends was always full of beer and food. Just a normal Mexican-American Rio Grande Valley home. Every Christmas, Thanksgiving and New Year's it was a celebration at my grandma's bar. Yes, my grandmother owned a bar. It was called "Race Café."

She even hosted horse races in the back of this bar. I actually spent many a Sunday at the horse races, with my mom and my aunt, Tia Nita, selling burgers and shakes to the horse racing spectating crowd. My grandmother made the best burgers. I remember it just being a fun time.

I remember my father taking me fishing a couple of times and even hunting at a ranch that his boss owned. I loved my father and I know he did his best to be a good dad. I remember really being proud of my father. He wasn't perfect but he definitely did the best he could with what he had.

CHAPTER 2
The Big City, Edinburg, Texas

About age twelve or thirteen I got introduced to marijuana and pornography. I remember my dad giving me sips of beer here and there. I saw my dad drink and smoke so I thought it was a cool thing to do. I remember starting to steal cigarettes from my dad's cigarette pack. Before you knew it I was smoking marijuana almost every day. Then my brother came home from the Navy and now I started smoking with him.

Then when I was fifteen years old my parents made the big move to Edinburg, Texas, the big city. Wow, a country boy in the big city. Or at least this is how it felt for me. At the time Edinburg was a town of about 50,000. But for a kid of fifteen that lived in the country all his childhood life, it was a big deal.

Now in the "big city" and in a new school things started to change very quickly. In my new school I was given the opportunity to choose from several options of elective classes. I remember really being excited because I was going to

9

be able to get into music and that I did. I joined the junior high choir. I remember thinking, "Wow, I am going to learn how to sing. This could be my big break. Maybe my dreams of being a rock star will become a reality after all." I was a dreamer. I remember going behind the Choir Hall to smoke weed and then going to class all stoned.

This is where I met my best friend Waldo. I was a "tenor" and Waldo was a "bass." We went everywhere together. We were the only rebels in our choir class. Waldo had an old 1956 Chevy truck. He was always working on it. It was a cool truck. Waldo was only fifteen and already had a driver's license. His parents were disabled so he had what was called a hardship driver's license. Waldo and I were inseparable. A little booze, marijuana and acid. The 80's were just around the corner and I was having the time of my life. But the so-called "good times" were about to take a turn for the worse.

It was the year 1979. Waldo and I, and another good friend of ours, Gilbert, decided we were going to skip school. So that morning we started smoking weed and walked down the road toward my house. I remember very clearly the thoughts that came to my head. To this day I don't know why these thoughts came to my head, I just know they did. We were walking by this house and I asked the guys if they wanted to break into that house, as I pointed with my finger. They both looked at me in disbelief and then said, "Let's do it." This was going to be the first time we ever broke into a house. We went in the house ransacked it, ate cereal, (we had the munchies) and stole a gun and some jewelry and went home. We all went to my house and just laughed about it all and said, "Wow, that was easy." This was the start of my criminal career.

For the next few weeks we started burglarizing homes, offices and buildings. We would break into homes and if there was a car we would take it with us and go joy riding. It was all just fun and games. Then we got caught. Both Waldo and I got indicted on felony charges of burglary of a building and burglary of a habitation. Both first-degree felonies.

I was only sixteen years old and considered a juvenile. So I was released to my parents but Waldo was already seventeen so he went to the county jail. I was only given probation but my friend Waldo was sent to prison for four months on what was called "shock probation." I really felt bad for my friend Waldo. But there was nothing I could do. Little did I know that my life was about to change forever.

CHAPTER 3

My Life Was About to Change Forever

On January 25th, 1980, I turned seventeen years old. I stopped breaking into houses after my friend Waldo went to prison but I didn't stop using drugs. I remember I used to like walking the streets. I would walk everywhere. One Friday evening my brother Pete, whom I shared a room with, had come home with a knife and he put it in the drawer. He told me not to get this knife because it wasn't his. But that night I was going to a dance with a friend of mine and I thought it would be cool to show him this knife.

I remember leaving the house that night and locking the door. I had already walked about a block away from the house when I decided I was going to go back for the knife. I actually had to climb through the window to get into the house. I had forgotten my key. I took the knife and started back on my way to the dance. I arrived about eight p.m. I spent a couple of hours there and then about ten p.m. I decided I was going to go back home. Like I said, I would walk the streets of Edinburg all the time. I was walking down Business Highway 281 and right in front of the HEB grocery store, this one guy offered me a ride. I didn't think much of it because I was always taking rides from people. I didn't see any difference this evening. So I hopped in the car and told him where to go.

But very quickly I sensed something was not right about this guy. He asked me if I wanted to smoke weed and said that he had some at his apartment. I told him no and to just take me home. I was now kind of scared and not sure what to do. Then he took off real fast in a whole different direction. I told him to let me off but he wouldn't stop the car. We wound up at this secluded place where he jumped out of the car and came around to my side.

My heart was pumping and I was afraid that he would find the knife I had on me and kill me or something. He came at me with a fury. This man wanted to sexually abuse me. I remember just trying to fight him off and we fell to the ground. He had me pinned down to the ground. I remember thinking, "This guy is going to kill me!" I remember reaching for the knife that I had hidden in my shoe and I stabbed him once. It all happened so fast. But he got off me. He ran into the fields around us and I ran to his car. I remember going straight home and not knowing what to do.

I finally woke up my parents and told them what had just happened. They told me that we needed to go to the police.

I remember my mom and dad telling me not to worry, that I wouldn't get in trouble because I was only defending myself. By the time we got to the police station they had already found the man that I had stabbed. He had died in the hospital.

I remember we were sitting in the police station, my dad, my mom and me. It was about one a.m. in the morning and the police officer came in and said these words, "Mr. and Mrs. Salinas, I am sorry to have to tell you this but the man that was stabbed just died in the hospital, and we are going to have to arrest your son for first-degree murder." I remember my heart just dropping. I could not believe what was happening to me. I was just defending myself. I didn't understand why I was being arrested. I was just a kid. My life was about to change forever.

They took me to the county jail. I was seventeen years old. I remember lying in my bed in the jail thinking, "What in the world is going on, how did this happen? Is this really happening?" I remember my mother and father coming to visit me, telling me, "Don't worry about anything, we're going to get you out of here." I remember my mother's words were very comforting. I knew my father loved me and I knew he would never let anything happen to me. But things didn't work out quite as we planned. I was told I was going to have to take it to trial. They were offering me fifty years in prison. It was like a soap opera, or a movie straight out of Hollywood. Picking the jury, talking to my lawyers and then finally going to trial. The day that verdict came, it was like a dream.

I remember the judge saying, "The jury has found the defendant guilty of first-degree murder." I remember my heart just dropping, again! Why was this happening to me? I was given a seventeen year sentence in prison. My attorneys immediately appealed the case. Thanks to my attorneys I was able to get out on an appeal bond. I became a very angry young man. I didn't understand how the "system" could be so cruel. I was only defending myself. I didn't mean to kill anybody. Now I was a convicted killer. How in the world did that happen to me?

CHAPTER 4
Learning the Ropes in the County Jail Time

Whether he is a sinner or not, I know not, one thing I know, that I was blind, now I see. (John 9:25)

In May 1980, seventeen years old, sitting in the county jail on a murder charge! At first it was hard, but I got used to being in jail. Plus, I knew that everything was going to be alright because my parents had hired a good attorney and I knew my dad wouldn't let anything happen to me. And besides I was only defending myself. I quickly learned the ropes to "doing time" and to my surprise, I halfway enjoyed it. I felt big and proud because I was "making it" with the "big dogs." "I can handle this," I would say to myself. "I can do this."

Within a couple of months, I met a thirty-five-year-old heroin addict named "Pancho." My first mentor. He came into our tank and he had to "break" — cold turkey! As the days passed by I got to know him and I became very good friends with him. He had tattoos all over his body and he spoke with authority, like he knew exactly what he was talking about. He was a three time loser and it seemed like everyone respected him, even the guards! And I decided that I wanted to be like Pancho!

Well, with "Pancho" in the house, things started rocking and rolling. Drugs started coming in, I got my first couple of tattoos and I even started earning respect from other inmates and guards. Pancho was teaching me the ropes and I was his right hand man. It was in here that I first got introduced to "the needle." Pancho got some heroin in and he "shot me up." I only did it once, but little did I know that this one time would one day come to haunt me. Well, the months passed by and my court date was getting closer. My girlfriend Maricela was even faithfully waiting for me, and my parents and lawyer would just tell me not to worry about anything. So, I didn't!

I remember this one "brother" that came in every week (into the jail tank) and spoke to us about Jesus. His name was Brother Vauhn, bless his heart! I had never heard the gospel presented the way Brother Vauhn had presented it to me and the seeds were planted. I did a few Bible studies, but I was not really enthused about this gospel stuff or this "new life" that they talked about. After all, I was doing just fine. I had everything I needed. I had commissary (my parents always sent me money). My girlfriend was waiting for me, my attorney was fighting for me, my family was encouraging and above all, I had "made it" behind the walls of confinement and I had earned my respect! What could possibly go wrong?!

Well, to make a long story short, I was convicted of murder and sentenced to seventeen years to the Texas Department of Corrections (now TDCJ). This was a devastating blow to me. I could not believe I had actually been convicted of something I felt justified for. Again, my parents and attorney had everything under control. I was told not to worry, that we would appeal the case and I would get out on an "appeal bond" pending the higher court's decision. And that's exactly what happened. My attorney appealed my case and I was released on an appeal bond.

Boy, what a feeling! I was FREE at last. I had no goals, no plans, no dreams and no sense of direction, but I was "FREE" and that's all that mattered to me.

For the next year or so I lived a free man. But like so many people in our society today, I had no idea what freedom really was, much less knew how to appreciate freedom. I became a very selfish and self-centered young man. I didn't care about anyone else but myself. My girlfriend was a great girl and she loved me, but I didn't care. I made her my wife, but I just wanted to use her and abuse her. I was ruthless. I treated her like trash. I was just a loser pot head. She did not deserve to be treated the way I treated her. God forgive me! But that's what loser men, like I was, do.

I would like to just stop here for a minute. If you are reading this book and you are a young father, PLEASE, I beg of you DO NOT abandon your children. Man-up!!! Make a decision to change! Be a father! Your children desperately need a father. More than you can even understand. Don't ruin your children's life. Get out of the gangs! Stop being a thug! Grow up. We already have enough loser fathers. What we need are fathers, husbands and leaders. "Being **male** is a matter of birth, being a **man** is a matter of choice." Take the challenge to become a man.

We lived with my parents and Maricela got pregnant. On January 27th, 1982, Karen Beth Salinas was born. What a beautiful child. I remember holding her in my arms and wondering, "What in the world am I going to do with my life? How in the world am I supposed to take care of this beautiful little girl?" But my life became a fantasy. I smoked marijuana and started drinking and doing acid. I lived in a fantasy world and my wife and daughter paid the price. I became more and more unfaithful to my wife; I hurt her and I didn't care. We had problems but I can honestly say today, they were all my fault.

I would like to say this before I go on. My daughter Karen Beth has always been very special and precious to me. Karen, if you ever read this, I pray to God that you find a way to forgive me for not being there, for not being a father. Apart from my mistakes and stupidity, I just didn't know how to love. I didn't know how to be a father. And as hard as it may be for you to believe me now, I do love you and always will! It took all this in my life, but I finally understood what love is!

On June 6th, 1982, after being on appeal bond for a year and a half, I was arrested on an aggravated robbery charge. I was nineteen years old. My life as I knew it came to a complete stop. I was a very selfish and confused young man. I had really messed up my life now. At first it was hard, but when I found out that I lost my appeal and I was told that I would be locked up for the next five to ten years, I just wanted to die.

I remember going to my bunk and just crying. I remember crying myself to sleep many a time. But I found strength somehow and I was determined to ride this thing out. Besides, I wasn't about to show myself weak in front of anyone in this place. And I didn't have God in my life, so I hardened my heart. I was told I was a convicted felon so I believed it and I started to live it. I told my wife to leave me, I told my family not to worry about me and I set out to make a name for myself behind these prison walls. It was a cold, cruel world. A world where only the strong survived. "Literally." I did things I would never have done in the free world. I even attempted to escape.

In September 1982, I was convicted for escape and aggravated robbery and sentenced to twenty years. It no longer "moved me." I was hard, I was cruel and I was mean. The words "I don't give a damn" were now my philosophy for living.

CHAPTER 5

Ferguson Unit "Little Alcatraz"

On November 10th, 1982, I hit "Ferguson Unit." A maximum security Texas prison. Ages ranging from fifteen to twenty-four years of age. They called it "Little Alcatraz." I remember walking in that place. It was something out of a horror movie. Everything within me wanted to run and get out of there, but there was no place to run. With everything bottled up inside of me and refusing to show any sign of fear, I took a deep breath and walked in to my assigned block, 12 Block.

I remember the door slamming behind me. What an awful feeling. I was there! The hour of truth! What would I do? How was I going to react? Well, to my surprise, I learned the ropes pretty quick! I had to. Evilness, hate, anger and prejudice abounded in this place. I was taught to hate anyone who was not of my race. Especially Black folks. And I did. I did everything in my power to build a reputation as a tough guy.

My race number one! "La Raza!" It was all about survival.

People got killed, people got raped, people got beat down and stabbed! It was a nightmare for some and just another day in the park for others. Here you had to kill, steal and destroy! The devil was destroying us and we couldn't see it. How very true.

By 1984 I had earned a reputation of being a die-hard leader. I was a "leader of the pack!" I had become stone cold hard hearted. The sensitivity of heart that I did have (and I believe all of us do have it) was well tucked away.

One day I got a new celly (cell-mate). We called him "99" because he had a 99 year sentence. He was a big guy, about 250-300 pounds. Well, he and I got along great. He was a mean cold-blooded person. One Saturday night we stayed up all night talking about all things we used to do, the things we were doing and the things we planned to do (Bad things). Well, we went to breakfast that Sunday morning about four a.m., came back and stayed up talking some more.

About six-thirty a.m. my celly, "99," started getting ready like he was going somewhere and I asked him where he was going. He said, "To church." I said, "To church?" He answered, "Yeah, I go every Sunday." He was a Catholic so he went to mass every Sunday like every other good Catholic. I thought about it and since I had never really seen that part of the prison, I decided to go "check it out." So at seven-thirty a.m., when they called church, we were out the door.

As we approached the chapel, I noticed that some people were going into the chapel and others were continuing straight into the school area of the prison, the education department. I asked my buddy "99" where those people were going and he said to Sunday school. Since I had been brought up in the Catholic faith, I knew what a mass was all about and I really considered it boring. So, I decided to go to Sunday school.

There was a Spanish-speaking brother greeting all the people coming in and telling the Spanish-speaking men that his class was in Spanish. So naturally I went there. At this point in my life I was not about to be seen or associated with any other race but my own. (Remember I was prejudiced, racist, and full of hate and anger. And let's not forget, ignorant and blind.)

After Sunday school we were led into the chapel for Christian services. Chaplain Kasner was the chaplain's name. I only remember that I sat and listened out of respect, but even today I can't remember what he preached about. All I remember is that somehow, someway this chaplain touched a part of me that I thought was untouchable! I remember hearing something about a new life and that I didn't have to live in hate and anger, loneliness and frustration. That there was a way out. That I could change my life! There was hope even behind these god forsaken, sin infested, demonic filled prison walls!

Like I said, I really don't remember what the sermon was about, all I know today is that, in that prison chapel, sometime at the beginning of 1984, that chaplain asked if anyone wanted to change, if anyone wanted to accept this new life, if anyone wanted to be forgiven for all their sins to come up and accept Jesus Christ in their heart and be changed forever! And for some unknown reason which I still have yet to understand, I went up there and gave my life to Jesus Christ.

For some weird reason I "believed" what this man was saying! I wanted to change but I just didn't realize that I could. Neither did I know how, much less that there was even a way to change. Today I understand that it was the love of God through the power of the Holy Spirit that touched me that day and I took the chance. A whole new world was opened to me. A world that I knew nothing about. The idea that I could actually change and be a better person became real to me that day. It was like I was waiting for someone to tell me that change was possible. A newfound hope was born in me that day. My life was about to change forever.

Chapter 6
A Newfound Hope

I didn't know too much about this newfound hope. All I was sure of was that I had been blind to this hope, but now I could see!

I walked back to my cellblock that day, convinced that something had happened to me. I wasn't sure what I was going to tell all my "homeboys," I only knew I was not the same. As I walked into my block with a Bible in my hand, my homeboys just looked at me crazy and one asked with a joking tone of voice, "Que onda Salinas, cristiano oh que?" (What's up, Salinas, are you a Christian now or what?) And I replied in a serious tone of voice, "Simon carnal, yo le voy a poner a la chorcha. Ya estuvo con migo." (Yes, man, from now on I am going to church. It's over for me.)

This was a big surprise to all my homeboys. They neither could believe it nor could they understand it. But one thing they knew and respected about me was that I didn't play games. When I made a decision, I meant it and followed through on it. So all my people (homeboys, friends and associates) respected my decision and just stood back and watched.

The Lord really started working in my life from the very start. That same Sunday night I got a re-assignment slip! I was put in school and moved into a trustee tank (block). I had been working in the fields for over two years now. I started attending church every Sunday and Wednesday. We were very fortunate to have a strong structured church. Our chaplain was very dedicated and we had a lot of dedicated brothers in Christ that really loved God.

I started growing and learning a lot. I was into every correspondent Bible course I could get my hands on. I watched other brothers whom I believed to be sincere and strong in their faith. If I was going to survive as a Christian then I had better learn what the Bible said about what I believed. So I stayed in the Bible. I listened, watched and learned.

Within six months I was deacon in our church. I had also been blessed with a job as the chapel janitor (back then called the chaplain ssi). My job was to sweep and mop the chapel. So I had access to the chapel and a lot of free time, and I spent it listening and watching preaching and teaching on video and cassette. I read many books and prayed many hours in that little chapel. I felt safe. I felt free!

This "religious" Bible stuff was making sense to me all because I dared to believe in the impossible! In the unthinkable! Not only believe in Christ for the salvation of my soul, but also to believe in the notion that I could actually be somebody outside of these prison walls. Not only to believe but actually have the spiritual tools and the know-how to actually do it! The same drive and enthusiasm that I had used to "make it" behind these walls of confinement, I was using to learn and come to know Him (Jesus) and the power of His resurrection. And I had found out that this is what I was supposed to do anyway. (Matt 22: 36-40) I was learning to see things in a godly perspective.

By 1986 I had become a pillar in the church. My life changing experience was not only being witnessed by the chaplain, other brothers and many of my old buddies, but prison officials were also convinced of my change. From the Sergeant to the Warden! I had found favor in the eyes of my peers, my Christian brothers and the very prison officials that once considered me a nobody and a trouble maker!

I was a walking miracle and they knew it and I knew it and God was getting all the Glory. By 1986 I was the Spanish speaking Sunday school teacher. I was our choir director. We had started dorm and block Bible studies and prayer groups. Many, many great things were happening, not only to me but also to people all around me. God was touching lives just like He had touched mine and I was excited to be part of that. God was using me and I didn't even realize it. With this in mind, let me say this: prison life is a very hard, cold and lonely thing to deal with. Many of us have to deal with the fact that we will have to spend many years here and for some, maybe not even see the "free world" ever again.

There's a lot of hurt, pain and depression that really embeds itself deep inside a person.

Some go crazy, others commit suicide and still others just become cold, emotionless and hard-hearted. And the sad part is we don't even see this happening to us. The hurt and pain are so intense sometimes, that we learn to numb our emotions and create a big hard shell around our hearts. Nothing coming in and nothing going out. If we ever knew how to use our emotions, the sensitivity diminishes. In essence, we are dead and don't even realize it. And not just the inmate himself — then you have the wives, children, sisters, brothers, moms and dads. Divorce, death in the family and more. The results of an incarceration can be devastating!

For me, thanks to my Lord and my willingness to obey and submit, things were great. Even though my wife, Maricela, had left me in 1985, I was still standing firm and trusting in God. I knew and believed beyond a shadow of a doubt that God had saved my life and had given me an ability I never knew I had.

CHAPTER 7

I Got Confused

I was twenty-three years old and I had been in prison for the past six years. Jesus had brought me a long way. I was no longer a problem; I was a problem solver. I had goals and dreams now. I was thinking wisely and godly now. The Lord Jesus had taken me from the very mists of sin and destruction; from being a young man with no hope, no dreams, no expectations, no kind of aspirations, no faith in God and full of hate and anger. Jesus took me and built me up and made me a new man, with new dreams, new expectations, and new aspirations. There was nothing I didn't believe I could do in Christ.

Brother Maxie was an elder in the church and Brother Soto, who was my friend and mentor, was the other elder. (There were two elders and ten deacons in the church leadership) Brother Soto and I became very close. In fact, Soto and I planned to get together in the free world and start our own business. Of course Brother Soto was the one with all the ideas. I just agreed with him and was willing to go through with our plans. Brother Soto finally went home.

What a glorious day after so many years in prison. Brother Maxie had already spoken to me about Brother Soto leaving and that I was the only deacon that was ready to take his place! "Me," Orlando Salinas, "an Elder." Just the thought of the responsibility of that office overwhelmed me.

Well, this next part of my life is hard to share, but I know I must. I got confused. I allowed Satan to put fear in my heart and I was led to believe that I neither was worthy nor would I be able to uphold such a high position in the church. How could I possibly carry out such an awesome responsibility? I knew the eldership was coming up and I didn't want to take the position. I couldn't take that position. So I was deceived into resigning from all my positions. I gave up my deaconship; I gave up being choir director; I placed another brother in the Spanish speaking Sunday School Class. In short, I stopped serving in the church.

I was deceived into thinking that I could just be a "regular" Christian. I figured in my mind that I would take this opportunity to go ahead and rid myself of all the responsibilities I was carrying. I figured it would be like taking a vacation from my work. After all, it wasn't like I was leaving the church or my faith! I loved God and I would never deny that. I had grown and learned a lot. I was very thankful. I wasn't hurting anyone anyway! (So I thought)

NOTE: Brother reading this, please don't ever make this mistake!

Don't let the devil deceive you. How foolish I was to believe that I had anything to do with what was freely given to me by God! He had brought me this far; what made me believe that now "I" was going to take over? Even if we do fail in areas, you just don't quit. You learn and go on. Proverbs says this: "The commandment is a lamp and the law is light and reproofs of instruction are the way of life."

I did continue going to church and I felt justified. I felt I had made the right decision. I felt comfortable. Little did I know that this decision was going to one day come back and "haunt me."

CHAPTER 8
Finally Free or So I Thought

Almost exactly one year after I resigned from serving in my prison church, I was released from prison. March of 1987. What a great day! My life had gone through so many changes and now it was time to prove myself. My family was eagerly awaiting my arrival and I had great plans. In my mind, nothing could stop me. I would go to school for A/C, get a job and then move to Houston. The Lord had blessed me with a drive to succeed that just wouldn't stop. I was a hard worker. I was confident. I was strong willed and I believed in myself.

To help me get started, my parents had bought me a brand new 1987 Ford pickup. My parents really did everything in their power to help me. My sisters and brothers supported me. (I only had one brother growing up, but when I was fifteen years old my parents adopted a five-year-old boy, so I've had two brothers most of my adult life.) I got a job with my dad and started going to school just as I planned. I was free at last and everything was going great. But not for long.

Just a few weeks after my release I was introduced to what would become the destruction of my life, "Cocaine." It seemed like everyone around me used this drug. It was like a fashion and it was very much in style. To my surprise, I met up with an old school buddy of mine who was into selling cocaine by the ounce and kilo and then I went into the business too. It was exciting at first. I mean, I held a job, went to school, had plenty of money and did whatever I wanted. I thought it was great. Life was great! I was on top of the world — nothing could stop me now!

But as the Bible tells us in Proverbs Chapter 12, Verse 15: "The way of a fool is right in his own eyes: but he that hearkeneth unto counsel is wise," and in Proverbs Chapter 14, Verse 12: "There is a way which seemeth right unto a man, but the end thereof are the ways of death."

It wasn't long before I met up with an old acquaintance, "the needle"! From the first time I tried it, I was hooked. It had only been three or four months since my release from prison and here I was, hooked on a drug that I had only seen in movies and heard others talk about. The thought had never even occurred to me that this drug, this white powder, this evil, evil substance I was dealing with could actually destroy my whole life. My dreams. My hope. Satan was about to have a field day with me. So when my habit got to the point that I thought I could no longer control it on my own, I turned to Mom!

I knew my mom could help me. Little did I know that my problem wasn't a family problem. It was much deeper and more evil and destructive that I could have possibly even started to comprehend. My mom was understanding and she did what she could. But she really didn't know what to do either.

By 1988 I finished school and I moved to Houston. My buddy, Brother Soto, was eagerly waiting for me. Our plans were finally coming together. He had already started his business and he was doing great. But I had become a startup drug addict. What I call a "loser" drug addict. I was a hard worker but all I could think of was party, party, party. Drugs, drugs, drugs.

I started working with Brother Soto and I started learning quickly. From ceramic tile installation to carpet to plumbing, to electrical to Formica and cabinetry. I even learned how to bid jobs.

Despite my drug addiction, I was determined to be successful. I had it under control. I was doing what most people said couldn't be done. Nothing could take me down. I was going against the odds and winning! Cocaine, beer and 80's music. What else could a man ask for?

My life revolved around work, work, work, party, party, party. I remember saying to myself, "As long as I have beer and cocaine, I will be happy." The relationships I had with women never mattered to me. As far as I was concerned, women come and go. They were just a part of life that really had no meaning to me, other than to be used by men. I was twisted in the head. I was a wicked man. I didn't care about anything else or anyone else. I was self-centered and selfish. I had no compassion for others and you know what? I didn't even realize it.

CHAPTER 9
I Met My Beautiful Wife

In July of 1989 I met my wife, Maria Isabel Mireles. I remember when I saw her for the first time I just thought she was the most beautiful girl I had ever seen. It was ten in the morning and I was sitting outside my apartment drinking a beer. (Ten a.m.? Beer?)

She was at the apartment swimming pool with her little niece and nephew, Jazmin and Alex. She was so beautiful, I thought to myself. Everything I could possibly hope for. I was convinced this was the girl for me. This is exactly what I need to get my life in order, a beautiful young wife. After my third beer I mustered up the courage to go talk to her. "Are those your kids?" I asked. And the rest is history. With her parents' consent, two months later, we got married. On September 22nd, 1989, she became Maria Isabel Salinas. I was in love!

I really was willing to do anything to make our marriage work. But what in the world did I know about marriage or love? I had never loved a woman in my whole life. And the time I thought I was in love, I was only twelve years old. But I did my best. I thought everything was going to work out great. I was smart, I was young, I had a good job, and I had a beautiful wife. What could possibly go wrong?

By 1990 I was self-employed. I had really gotten the hang of this remodeling business so I quit working for my friend and decided to start my own little business. I made good money but it never seemed to be enough because I was a loser drug addict. I jumped from one great idea to another. We (my wife and I) also jumped from one home to another. "Things will get better," I would always tell Isabel. And my precious wife would never say a word; she just encouraged me and supported me.

One night I was out on a binge and I no longer had money to buy drugs. I decided I was going to go steal cocaine from some drug dealers I knew. It sounds crazy now that I think about it but that's how drug addicts like me think. Well, that didn't work out too good for me. I barely got out alive. I remember someone putting a gun to my head as I was sitting in my truck. It all happened so fast. All I remember doing is stepping on the gas.

The next thing I heard was gunshots and I felt a warm/cold sensation in my back. I had gotten shot right on my spinal cord. I made it to the hospital and by the grace of God, although the bullets hit me, they didn't penetrate enough to do significant damage. The doctor said that had the bullets penetrated far enough I would have been paralyzed for life.

Do you know what's that called? The grace of God. Even this near death experience didn't stop me from my crazy, drug addicted life.

My drug addiction started to really take its toll on our lives. My wife even joined me in my addiction. I guess she just wanted to feel a part of my world. I was alienating her from my life because of drugs and didn't even know it. I always "assumed" she was ok.

She soon started nagging me more and more about my drug and alcohol habits. So I did what any other coward would do, I RAN.

This was 1992 and my wife was pregnant. By this time my ex-wife, Maricela, and I had been in contact and we were talking about getting back together. I actually just felt very guilty for how I had treated her in the past. And of course she was the mother of my daughter Karen.

Well, I decided to leave my pregnant wife and get back together with Maricela. I really loved my wife and I never wanted to hurt her or leave her, but I was running. And crazy. And selfish!! (The root of all our problems: selfishness) And when you are addicted to drugs and alcohol like I was, you do not make wise decisions. You make very stupid, selfish, "all about you" decisions. We like calling them "mistakes" to make ourselves feel better. You do things in the sense of what feels better instead of what's right.

At this point in my life I was very confused. I couldn't keep a job. I was living with family members. My wife was pregnant. So I ran. My ex-wife even came down from California to see me. And we spent a couple of weeks together! She loved to smoke weed and she didn't mind my drugs so we hit it off just fine. I was very confused!

CHAPTER 10

Moving Back Home to Mom. It Only Gets Worse, Never Better

Thanks to my precious wife who fought our separation from the beginning, I didn't get back with my ex-wife and decided to reunite with my pregnant wife and move back to my hometown, Edinburg, Texas. My mom took us in and we were going to start a new life.

(By the way, this is where most loser drug addicts like me wind up, at Mom's!! Or Tia's, or Grandma's or whoever will take them in.)

I was happy, my wife was happy and we were off to a new beginning, again! By now, I knew I had a deep-rooted problem, but I was convinced I could handle it. Jumping from one job to another. Always trying something new.

A good friend of mine that I met in Houston, Adolfo, came down to the Valley with me and we joined forces. We became partners and started our own business, Custom

Remodeling. We made a great team. Things were great. We moved out of my parents' home and into a three-bedroom house. A room for my wife and me, a room for Adolfo and his wife, and the other room was made into our office. My partner and I went fifty-fifty on all expenses and earnings, but he always had more money than me. In fact, I always owed him money. The more money I made, the more I spent. Drugs and alcohol were really taking their toll. My addictions seemed to get worse and worse. I even started stealing from my own family.

By 1994 I sought help for my addiction for the first time. But it was only to make my wife happy. By now I'd been out of prison and on parole for seven years. I had accomplished everything I set out to accomplish, but for some reason I couldn't progress anymore. I was just spinning my wheels and didn't understand why. I always blamed it on not making enough money. Never the drugs.

After this first attempt at getting treatment, it seemed like things just got worse. My family was always on my case. My wife got a job. Our first daughter, Andrea, was born and I just sank deeper and deeper into my addiction. I even tried going to church. That only helped to clear my conscience but my addiction always resurfaced. By now I was really wondering why I couldn't control myself. My life was falling apart and I just couldn't get a grip on life. My family and friends were losing respect for me. Everyone else could see I had a problem but me.

The treatment centers only convinced me that everyone else had problems, not me. My wife pleaded with me so many times, but I just couldn't get my head together. My whole life was literally falling to pieces and I hated the fact that I could not do anything about it. My addiction led me to lie and cheat more and more. I'd sell and pawn tools and equipment at a blink of an eye. My arms would be full of needle marks and I still couldn't get ahold of myself. All I could think of was "Where am I gonna get my next hit?" It had become a vicious, wicked cycle. My partner and I finally parted ways because of my addiction.

By 1996 my life was a total mess! My wife was pregnant again and Aolani (Lani) was born on August 7th, 1996. I was ruthless, heartless, and hopeless. I had lost my house, we were living with my parents again and everyone knew I had a very serious drug addiction. The only person holding my life together was my precious wife. And that was only to the best of her ability. Family and friends had lost all respect for me. The little bit of work that I did do, I used the money for my drug habit. I wanted so much to change! To turn back the hands of time, but I just couldn't. I knew with everything inside of me that nothing or nobody could possibly come close to helping me. I was beyond human help!

My precious wife tried and tried. She cried, she begged, she did everything in her power to help me and understand me. Even when I stole from her, pawned her jewelry and continually lied to her, she still tried to help me. I just wanted to die. I even contemplated suicide several times because I thought my family would probably be better off without me. I was a loser father, a loser husband and a loser son.

By the end of 1996, I had no job, no tools, no truck and no self-respect. I had pawned everything I owned. And more. I was full of guilt, hurt, shame, pain, confusion, condemnation and self-pity. The only thing that would take me out of this depressing world of mine was cocaine.

I knew what was wrong with me.

I had left God behind me a long time ago. I knew He was the only one that could help me. But I just couldn't get ahold of my God! And besides, what could God possibly do with my messed up, broken life anyway? I was about to find out thanks to my uncle Benjamin "Jamin" Dominguez.

He would always come and invite my wife and me to church. Every Sunday morning there he was, dropping by just to see if we'd like to go. I'd tried going to church before. I had even joined the Victory Outreach Program for a few months, but I always wound up in the same place. Drug addiction! Sin and disobedience had engulfed me and entangled me to the point of total destruction. I was like a fish out of the water. Totally helpless and totally hopeless! Hopeless, hopeless, hopeless. *Have you ever been hopeless?*

CHAPTER 11

My Daughter's Fourth Birthday

In December of 1996 I walked through the doors of "The Door Christian Fellowship," McAllen, Texas. It was a little church of about fifty or so people. It was on the corner of 10th and Freddy Gonzales Drive. Gabriel Alonso was the Pastor. He was an on fire Holy Ghost preacher. The people were friendly and I really enjoyed the pastor.

I remember going up to the altar after one message and begging God to help me. I desperately wanted to change my life but I couldn't. My drug addiction was so engraved in my very soul that even on my knees, in the front of that church asking God for help and deliverance, my mind was still wondering, "Where am I going to get my next hit!" I was a dead man walking. That's what drug addiction does, it kills the very soul of man. It's called sin.

The New Year rolled around and I remember the first week or so of January 1997. I was up front on my knees at the altar again with my wife on one hand and my daughter

Andrea on the other (Lani was at the church nursery). I remember crying out to God for a touch! I remember totally just giving up. I remember telling God to take me out of my misery. I told God "TO DO WHATEVER IT TOOK" to deliver me from this wicked addiction and lifestyle I had created for myself. Well, God in His mercy and grace heard my cry. My wife and I were about to enter the "trial" of our life: My daughter's fourth birthday.

Two weeks after that last day in church, I was in jail. I had robbed a store, again, on my daughter's birthday. I was indicted on a first degree felony, aggravated robbery, on a habitual indictment. I was on my way back to prison for the rest of my life.

It was Saturday night, January 17th, 1997. The next day, January 18th, was my daughter Andrea's fourth birthday. I was sitting in the living room watching TV. Can you guess what I was thinking? My wife, Isabel, and my two daughters, Aolani and Andrea, were in the bedroom. My wife comes out of the bedroom and tells me, "Please watch the kids. I am going to take a shower. Please don't go anywhere."

She gets in the shower and guess what I did? Before I left, I went and "looked" for her purse, stole her last twenty dollars and took off. Walking, of course. I was a loser. I didn't even have a bike. I had pawned everything including my truck. I was a loser. I was so ashamed of my worthless self that I just wanted to die. After buying ten dollars worth of cocaine, a couple of beers and some cigarettes, I walked the streets throughout the night desperate for more drugs, beer, cigarettes, more of anything. I was ashamed to go back home. I had no one or no place to go. So I went back to my drug dealer's house but he wasn't home.

I waited there for him till four in the morning. When he drove up, he knew who I was and what I wanted. He got out of the car half drunk and just threw me a twenty dollar bag of cocaine. I immediately went to the back room and fixed up my syringe. I put it in my arm and the unthinkable happened! I missed!!!

It was a dark room and I only had a lighter for light. So when I put the needle in my arm I missed the vein. Only a loser drug addict like me will understand what that means. It means the cocaine didn't go into my veins so I didn't get high. And for a drug addict like me, that is like the end of the world. Something happened in my mind that night that was pure wickedness. I became so enraged I remember saying to myself, "I am going to get another hit and I don't care who I have to kill."

I made up my mind that I was going to go rob a store and I knew exactly which one. The 7-11 on the west side of town. So I walked across town and got to the 7-11 close to six a.m. It was now Sunday morning, my daughter's fourth birthday.

It is almost six a.m. and I am standing in front of that 7-11. I've been out all night long. I am debating with myself: "Do I rob the store and risk going to prison for the rest of my life or do I just go home?" There is a big digital clock across the street and it says five-fifty-eight. "In two minutes," I think to myself. "I'm going to go in at exactly six a.m." My heart and mind are racing. I am thinking of all the things I've done in my life. All the messed up things I have done. The stealing, the cheating, the lying, and manipulating. The people I've hurt, the pain I have caused my family and friends.

How did I ever get myself in this mess!

How did I become such a hard-core loser drug addict? I just wanted to die! I didn't care anymore. In my mind I knew this was exactly what sin does — it destroys not only your life but it destroys the lives of the people around you. The people you say you love the most. It's amazing how the devil works. Destroys your very soul. I was just a dead man walking. The truth was that I had died a long time ago. I'd been putting needles in my arm for ten years now. Just a few hours earlier I had stolen my wife's last twenty dollars. She was going to use that money today for my daughter's fourth birthday. I was just a loser!! I was worthless — a loser father, a loser husband, and a loser son! I was hopeless!

The clock turned to six a.m. I made my decision. I ran into the store and put my hand in my pocket and pretended like I had a gun. I yelled at the clerk, "Give me the money! Give me the money!" The cashier gave me sixty dollars and I grabbed the money and ran out the door. I was going to my drug dealer's house. I knew what I had just done. If I got caught I was going to prison for the rest of my life. I was going to go get sixty dollars worth of cocaine, shoot it all up and just kill my worthless self.

I remember running to an old neighbor I used to live by and I told her some crazy story about my truck being stranded and I asked if I could use her phone. I called a taxi and my drug dealer and I told him I was on my way for more cocaine. The taxi came but we didn't get very far. Just three blocks away the Edinburg PD stopped the taxi. I ran out of the taxi and tried to escape but it was no use. I was surrounded and was tackled by the officers. It was over. I knew what I had just done. I was on my way to prison for the rest of my life.

SOME PICTURES OF MY JOURNEY

Thank you Nottingham, Walsall, WestBromwich, Smethwick!! UK we ♥ you!!

Orlando and his wife, Isabel, in the UK.

Orlando speaking at a school in Harlingen, Texas.

Orlando in Romania.

Orlando Street preaching in the Philippines.

Orlando preaching in a prison in Guam.

His wife and daughters visit him in prison, the Segovia Unit, Edinburg, Texas.

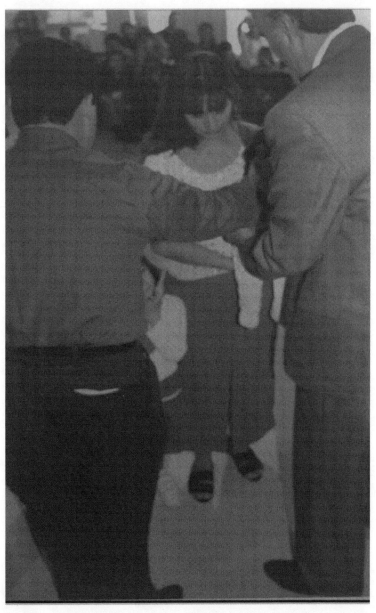

Orlando's wife Isabel dedicating their daughters to the Lord after he was sent to prison in 1997. The Door church on 10th and Freddy, Pastor Gabriel Alonso and Evangelist Frank Escobar.

July 2003, the day Orlando came home from prison after doing 6 1/2 years.

Police beat

Baytown man shot in back

The truck Orlando was in when he got shot at 9 times.

Attempted escape news paper clip.

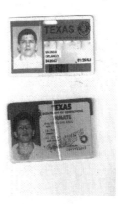

Orlando two prison ID's.

Orlando preaching in his home church in McAllen, Texas.

Orlando's restored family today (2018). His two daughters and sons-in-laws, granddaughter, wife, and son.

Left to right: Beto, Lani, Orlando, Gwen (granddaughter), Isabel, Andrea, William, Ozzy (Center).

Orlando preaching in a Texas prison.
(Segovia Unit Edinburg, TX)

Orlando speaking at a school in Guam.

CHAPTER 12
Aggravated Robbery

By seven o'clock Sunday morning, January 18th, I was sitting in the Edinburg police station charged with aggravated robbery! I was indicted with a habitual indictment on a first degree felony. One part of me felt relief and the other just wanted to die! I remember just crying out to God in that city jail and just telling God that I didn't care if I had to go to prison for the rest of my life but to please help me change that monster in the mirror. I didn't even try to call home. By noon I was already in the county jail.

It was my daughters fourth birthday and I felt so ashamed. I knew I had to call my wife to let her know something but I didn't want to call. I waited till five p.m. and I made that infamous call and here is how that call went. I said, "Babe," (that's a drug addict for you, still calling her babe) "I am not coming home anymore. I really messed up this time." I could hear my daughter Andrea in the background saying, "Is that Daddy, Mom? Is that Daddy?" And the next thing I hear is this little voice that said, "Daddy, Daddy, today was my birthday and you weren't here, where were you? Are you coming now?"

I remember that day like it was yesterday. I already wanted to die, but when I heard those words, my whole world came crumbling down on me like you have no idea. My legs buckled and I fell to my knees. I just broke down in tears of desperation. Men there in the county jail just watching me but I didn't care. What have I done? I had just destroyed my life and the life of my family. I was completely hopeless and there was nothing I could do.

Have you ever been hopeless? Has your world ever come crumbling down on you? For the first time in my life I realized what was supposed to be the most important part of my life. MY FAMILY! My children. What a realization, what a revelation. The pain and the hurt were so overwhelming; it was too much for one person to bear. I just wanted to die! I had ruined my life and brought my family down with me. Back in jail, with no money and no source of comfort.

My family had given up on me. There was nothing they could do for me anymore. I was hopeless, afraid and angry. Nothing or nobody could possibly relieve me of this hopelessness and despair. There was nothing I could say or do to change what had happened in my life and what I had done to my family. The people I had hurt! The people I had let down! What was I to do? I knew what I needed to do. In fact,

I knew He was the only one that could help me! Without me realizing it, tragedy and hopelessness had led me right into the arms of Jesus!

In the very midst of my hopelessness and despair, God was reminding me of His love for me. Telling me that though the whole world is against me, He was on my side. My mind and heart started remembering scriptures. "If you believe all things are possible to him who believes…When you are weak then I am strong…I shall never leave you or forsake you…The weapons of our warfare are not carnal but mighty through God…" I remembered the scripture in Deuteronomy 30:19 (back then I didn't remember where it was, but I knew what it said).

Today I know it was the Holy Ghost that brought it back to my heart. "I call heaven and earth as witnesses today against you, that I have set before you life and death, blessing and cursing; therefore **choose life** that both you and your family may live." Rays of hope started shining into my desperate wicked heart. Fighting the hurt, pain, loneliness and condemnation I felt. I had no idea how God could possibly make things better for me. I just knew I had to make a decision.

I was once asked why I turn to God now and told that I should have turned to God when I was in the free world.

My answer to that is simple, "Who else do you turn to when you're hopeless?"

Today I realized I didn't need to know how. On my knees beside my bunk in that county jail, in tears, I committed my life to Jesus Christ, again. Against all odds, with no strings attached, *I chose to believe in the impossible*. I asked Jesus to come into my heart and help me change! Not to get me out of jail, but to deliver me from that monster in the mirror! That monster I had become! And the transformation began!

CHAPTER 13

The First Day in Court

My wife and daughters lived with my mom. I had left her with no money, no transportation, and no hope and in debt. She had a husband that had caused her so much pain and now he was in jail with no hope of coming home anytime soon. I was facing twenty-five years to life because of the habitual indictment. I had no lawyer, no money to hire one and very little support from my family (for which I could not blame them). And things didn't seem to get any better. But I thank God for that little church on 10th and Freddy, *The Door Christian fellowship*.

My wife had gotten saved and started attending church more regularly. She found support through the sisters in the church. Both my wife and I started seeking our God. We were both in a hopeless situation, but we both decided to "choose life" in Christ. Our faith grew stronger and stronger with each passing day. For some crazy reason we chose to believe that our God was going to see us through this. Despite all the opposition against us, we continued to believe in victory. And the oppositions were many: with a court appointed attorney, a judge that wasn't too happy with my criminal background, two parole officers that were against me, a habitual indictment and a parole violation, things did not look good at all.

I remember the first day of court and things just got worse. My court appointed attorney told me he would do what he could to help me and said he would try to get me a minimum sentence. A minimum sentence for my case was twenty-five years. Sitting in that court room, I watched my attorney get up and start his opening statements. He began with, "Your Honor, we are going to ask the court to consider a minimum sentence in this case."

As soon as he said "minimum sentence" Judge Leticia Hinojosa looked up and said, "Counselor, hold it right there." Then she turned and looked at me and said, "Mr. Salinas, please step up to the bench." This is what judges will do when they want to talk very seriously to you. She asked me, "You are on parole, is that correct?"

I said, "Yes, Ma'am." (I had been on parole all these years.)

She looked down at the paper work in front of her and she said, "Mr. Salinas, you are on parole, and you went to prison for burglary of a building, burglary of a habitation, murder, aggravated robbery, escape and now another aggravated robbery?" And she turned to my attorney and said, "And you want me to consider a minimum sentence?" She said, "Counselor, it is going to be very difficult for you to convince me to even come close to a minimum sentence," and she reset my court hearing for a later date. This is what I was facing, on my daughters fourth birthday in 1997. I was hopeless.

After months of hearings and postponements, a pre-sentencing report was presented with a fifteen year sentence recommendation to the court. At least this was better than a twenty-five year sentence. A fifteen year sentence would mean I would have to serve seven and a half years before even being "considered" for parole. As I stood before Judge Leticia Hinojosa, I didn't know what to expect. But nobody expected what was about to happen.

To the surprise of my attorney, myself and everyone in that courtroom, the judge did something amazing. She called me up to the bench and she said,

"Mr. Salinas, I want you to know that if I see you in my courtroom ever again, you can be sure that I will send you to prison for the rest of your life. But after much thought and consideration, and to be totally honest with you I am not even sure why I am doing this today. But here's what I am going to do, I am going to sentence you to a six and a half-year sentence."

I could not believe what I had just heard! A miracle right before our eyes. I could not believe what had just happened. If you are reading this and you have been asking God for a sign or a miracle, He just sent you one.

CHAPTER 14

On My Way Back to Prison

I chose to believe in the impossible and the miracle happened for me. Wow! I couldn't believe my ears when Judge Leticia Hinojosa looked me straight in the face and said, "Mr. Salinas, I don't know why I am going to do this but I am going to sentence you to six and half years." It was a miracle right before my eyes! The impossible had just happened.

I was on my way back to prison with a six and a half-year sentence and I was excited!! Yes, that's what I said, "excited"!! I wasn't excited about going back to prison, I was excited because I knew that a six and a half-year sentence was a miracle from God. Some called it "luck." I choose to believe it was a miracle. I had stood before one of the toughest judges in the district, with a long criminal history that started when I was fifteen. I was now thirty-three years old, indicted on a habitual indictment, on a first degree felony and the judge only gives me six and half years. I repeat: some people call it luck. I choose to call it a miracle.

For this reason, I have become eternally grateful for God's amazing grace.

Special note to the prisoner:

Let me take a minute here and speak to those of you in prison or on parole at this moment in your life.

If you are reading this book right now and you know that you should be dead or in prison, then you should be eternally grateful as well. Maybe you are in prison and you know that you should have gotten more "time" than what you got. You too should understand the amazing grace of God. But I have a question for you: are you grateful? Or have you forgotten what the Lord your God has done for you? Or are you still just as selfish and self-centered as you've always been? Do you lie to your family and make them feel sorry for you just so they will send you money? Are you even trying to change your life? What are you doing with your miracle? What are you doing with your second chance in life? Do you want to change your life? I mean really, do you really want to change your life? Because if the answer to this question is YES, then I can help you. Keep reading. Let me tell you exactly how I did it.

With a six and a half-year sentence and a renewed spirit of hope, I was now focused on "doing my time" and doing whatever I needed to do to change my life. Against all odds I made a decision that I was going to change my life and I didn't care who I had to "kill"!! And guess "who" I had to kill? The monster in the mirror.

See, this isn't rocket science. Most people know exactly what they need to do. But the doubts quickly started settling in. I wasn't sure where to start or what to do? "Who am I kidding anyway?" I would think to myself. "Do I really think I could change my worthless self? Is that even possible? Who do I turn to? Who do I trust?" These are the "voices" in my head that haunted me for years.

I use to cry myself to sleep just thinking about the things that I had done. All the hurt I had caused my family and friends. I honestly thought about giving up many times. I really could not conceive the idea that a loser like me could ever amount to anything in life. Not after everything I had done.

But let me tell you what kept me going. It was another voice, it was that little voice that echoed in my head almost on a daily basis. "Daddy, Daddy, today was my birthday and you weren't here, are you coming now?" I still remember it like it was yesterday. The pain, the regret and the hopelessness was so overwhelming, I just wanted to die.

I had ruined my life and broken the heart of my little girl. She believed in her daddy and her daddy let her down. How do you change that??? This is why I am so grateful for the miracle working power of God, Who is able to take what the devil meant for evil and turn it into good. I wasn't sure how God could turn this situation around, but I chose to believe in the impossible!!! That little voice kept me believing. It kept me believing. Sometimes I would literally *force myself* to believe!!!! Let me say that again, "I FORCED myself to believe!!!"

CHAPTER 15

Garza West? Back in the Texas Prison System
I had a plan

I had a plan. I figured the first thing I would do as soon as I got into the Texas prison system again, was to enroll in college and start working on some sort of degree. Remember, I had been in the Texas prison system back in the 80's so I knew that they offered college and I was going to take full advantage of it.

In1998 I was shipped off to a place called Garza West. I had never heard of Garza West. What in the world is Garza West? Well, I was soon to find out.

The Texas prison system had changed dramatically since the 1980's. It was like night and day. The guards were different, the environment felt different. It just seemed so different. I'll never forget my first day in "Garza West." I walked into my dorm with my little duffle bag of belongings and

73

found my bunk. Then some idiot walks up to me and asks, "Who are you running with?" I said, "What? What are you talking about?" I wasn't sure what he was asking me. Then he went on to explain his little game, how I needed to choose what gang or group of people I would represent.

Then I went on to explain my little game. I told him, "Look, dude, I don't know what you are talking about and I don't care. I am a Christian man. I am going to change my life. I am going to the top!!!" Now I don't know if it was my tattoos or the Holy Ghost, but I choose to believe it was God. They never bothered me again.

I was told that I would be here for at least the next two years. And to my surprise there were no college classes available at this prison unit. This really bummed me out because I was really looking forward to enrolling in college ASAP. "What do I do now?" I thought to myself. But the answers soon came in the prison library. I tell people all the time, "My life change started in a prison library." They just look at me like some of you reading this are thinking right now, "What? A prison library? What does that mean?" Glad you asked.

My plan was to put myself through college and educate myself. But there was no college available. So I did the next best thing. I decided to start going to the prison library and start reading. I figured that I could at least work on my vocabulary and improve my communication skills. I had the street and the prison lingo down pat. But remember I wanted to change my life. I didn't want to be a "vato loco (crazy man) for Jesus." I knew my vocabulary had to change so I just thought reading would be the best way to do that.

Little did I know that "reading" was going to take me to a whole new world that I did not know existed. The world of "personal development." I tell people all the time, Jesus Christ "saved" my life, but books "changed" my life. And that they did.

CHAPTER 16

The Process of Change Begins I Learn Two New Words:
Personal Development

I f you want to change your life, you are going to have to read. And learn to read the right books. There is no getting around this. You MUST read "If" you want to change your life. Every great leader, business person or preacher is a reader. "Not all readers are leaders, but all leaders are readers." I remember thinking to myself, "If I am going to be reading I may as well try to learn as much as I can." I had started thinking about maybe one day having my own business. So I started looking for anything that had to do with business.

I remember reading books on marketing, financing, real estate and management. One day as I was looking through the books in the library, I found this book that really jumped out at me. I felt like I had found gold. And I knew it was God helping me just by the title alone. It was called *The Complete Idiot's Guide to Starting Your Own Business*. I couldn't believe it. I thought, "Wow!! Thank you, Jesus, a book written just for me." I was an idiot!!! I was so excited about this book. This book really helped me get the right perspective on business. It gave me not only the right frame of mind but it gave me a road map to starting my own business.

Then one day I found another book that jumped out at me. It was called *Awaken the Giant Within* by Tony Robbins. Now this book taught me two new words and led me into a world that I did not know existed, the world of "personal development." The more I read, the more I wanted to learn. I remember I started carrying a book and a dictionary everywhere I went. I became obsessed with learning new words, changing my vocabulary and this idea of personal development.

I wondered why I had never heard about this before. I remember reading a book by Zig Ziglar, *Over the Top*. This is where I got the term, "I am going to the top" and the idea of the "rolling university." Learning and personal development became my passion. Jesus Christ had "saved" my life and now "books" were helping "change" my life!

I didn't realize it at the time but this prison unit, Garza West, became the foundation of my life change. I started getting involved in every church service available to me. We used to have church services in the gym. I became a chaplain's helper. We were the ones that would set up the chairs for every church service or event we had. I started a prayer group everywhere I went. God was moving in my life and I was excited.

God continued to be faithful to my wife as well. She had surrendered her whole life to God's will for her life and became a faithful member of her church, *The Door, McAllen, Texas*. She would always tell me about all the things they were doing and how she loved going to church. We both believed that God had a plan for us. We were not sure how everything was going to turn out but we both continued to believe in the impossible for our life, our future and our two daughters, Andrea, and Lani.

God was faithful. And the process of change had begun. I spent two years in Garza West and in the year 2000 I was shipped off to Ellis Unit.

CHAPTER 17
Death Row, Ellis Unit

Ellis Unit is one of the oldest Prison Units in Texas. It was built in 1965 about twelve miles north of Huntsville, Texas. It was designed to house all the Texas Death Row inmates (Men who had been sentenced to death) and was considered one of the toughest Prison Units in Texas. The year I got there (2000), they had started moving all death row inmates to another prison unit. Too many inmates had already tried to escape and they were trying to make the prison safer.

This was an interesting experience for me. I met a lot of men who had been there for many years. You are talking about fifteen, twenty, twenty-five years and more. I had several "lifer" friends who were never getting out at all. One of these was Rene from Pharr, Texas. He was a Christian brother, and he had been there in Ellis Unit for thirty years. No, that's not a typo. I said thirty years. He had come up for parole about twelve times and they kept on denying him a parole release. Crazy.

Ellis Unit would be my home for the next eighteen months. This unit had its own chapel and a Chaplain that ran a strong Christian program. All kinds of Bible studies and classes. It reminded me of when I was in prison the first time, in the 1980's, on Ferguson Unit, not only because of the Christian environment but this prison was designed or structured exactly the same way Ferguson Unit was.

There were a lot of "on fire" Christian brothers here. I went to church services all the time and became friends with many of the Christian brothers and leaders in the church.

I believe I grew and matured a lot in my Christian walk on this unit. You see, in prison you are confronted with a lot of different religions. You are talking about Catholics, Baptists, Methodists, Jehovah's Witnesses, Mormons, Muslims and the list goes on. My faith and my doctrine were challenged and tried. I must admit there were some that almost convinced me of their "religion" or their way of thinking. But I was a man of prayer, I was on a mission for "Truth," and God was faithful.

So if you are reading this book and you are confused about what to believe, let me just say this. There is absolutely nothing that can compare to JESUS CHRIST and the power of His resurrection. I call Him the miracle worker. So if you need a miracle in your life, I only know one miracle worker. His name is Jesus Christ.

I had to make some serious decisions on what I was going to believe. What was truth to me? I already knew how to be a Christian in prison. But in the back of my mind I knew the greatest challenge still lay ahead. Could I really handle the "free world"? Sometimes I had to force myself to believe.

God continued to be faithful to my wife and me.

Another great thing about Ellis Unit was that it offered colleges courses and a bigger library, both of which I was very excited about. I continued to read and study and really began to think about my future. I was halfway through my prison sentence so I started to seriously plan out what exactly I wanted to do with my life. I decided that starting my own business was what I was going to do. So I started planning for that.

I read many business books and personal development books that really helped me set goals and plans. My work experience had mainly been home remodeling work so I decided that I was going to start a remodeling company specializing in kitchen and bathroom renovations. I even wrote a business plan for this. I remember always thinking of names for my business. I had gathered a list of about fifteen different names but the one that stood out the most was "Custom Quality Renovations." I really liked this name, but in my mind I wanted people to know exactly what I "specialized" in as soon as they saw my business card, which was kitchen and bath renovations. I also wanted the words "remodeling specialist" in the name somewhere.

After months of deliberation on what name to use, a friend of mine came up with a brilliant idea (Well, at least I thought it was brilliant). His name was Joel. He said, "Why don't you take the first letter of each word in 'Custom Quality Renovations' and put them in front of the words 'Kitchen and Bath Renovations'? In other words, 'CQR Kitchen and Bath Renovations.'" This sounded great but the words "Remodeling Specialist" were still missing. So then *"CQR Kitchen & Bath Remodeling Specialists"* was born.

Today if you Google "Kitchen and Bath Remodeling Edinburg Texas" my company dominates the first page of Google. Wow! Who would have thought a loser drug addict like me could ever amount to anything? It's called the mercy and grace of God and "Believing in the impossible" is the key.

CHAPTER 18
Segovia Unit

The Ellis Unit was a great experience for me. Can you imagine that? Prison being a great experience? I truly believed that God had a plan for my life. I wasn't sure what but I continued to "choose" to believe in great things.

I am telling you, it's a choice. Overcoming in life is a choice! Having a great experience in prison is a choice! Success is a choice! A choice, I am telling you.

I had been in prison for over four years now. My precious wife would sacrifice about every six months to come see me in Ellis Unit. When I was in Garza West it was only two and a half hours from where my wife lived so she would come every other month to see me. But Ellis Unit was eight hours away, so that made it more difficult and expensive. But God in His mercy was about to show Himself faithful, again!! What amazing grace.

The year was 2001. I'll never forget that hot summer night. I was in my cell lying down on my bunk trying to stay cool, with the air from my little six-inch prison fan hitting my face. It was about eleven p.m., lights were out. Then the boss man (The Guard) came to my cell and said, "Salinas, what's your number?" I said, "343543." I thought he was just counting because that was about the time they would do the count. In prison they count about eight to ten times a day. But then he said, "Pack it up. You're on chain."

When you hear the words, "Pack it up. You're on chain," what they are saying is for you to pack up all your belongings because you are being moved to another prison unit. I remember jumping off my bunk and asking him, "Where am I going?" He said, "Segovia Unit!"

I couldn't believe my ears! I was so excited I stood in front of my cell and yelled out, at the top of my voice, "Thank you, Jesus, thank you, Jesus, I am going home!!!" Everybody thought I was crazy but I didn't care. I was going home and I knew it was God. You can call it luck or anything else you want to call it. But I "choose" to believe it was God making Himself real in my life and in the life of my family. What a mighty God we serve.

Segovia Unit is a prison in my home town of Edinburg, Texas. It sits just north of Edinburg and it was only five miles from where my wife and my two daughters were living. Now my family would be able to come see me every weekend. I was going to be able to see my daughters more and build a stronger relationship with my wife.

Getting to Segovia unit was so exciting. The very next weekend my wife and daughters were there to visit me. My wife and kids were so happy and excited all the time. My wife and I knew that it was all the grace of God in our life. God was showing Himself faithful and we were forever grateful.

I only had two more years to go and I would be home. My heart and mind were full of hopes and dreams. Segovia Unit also turned out to be an amazing experience of personal growth and maturity for me. I kept going to the library, kept reading and learning. I stayed involved in church and continued to plan for my future. I took a computer class and every other class I needed to take before my release (Changes and voyager for example).

I remember this one class I took where I caught the vision of manhood and how desperately we needed "men" in our society. Every Thursday a brother from an outside church would come and bring in a video series from a man named Edwin Luis Cole. These were some powerful teachings and this is where my burden, my mission for reaching out to men who were going through what I experienced was born.

I started learning and hearing things I had never heard before. About how to be a father, a husband and a leader. This is where I got the idea or the concept that *"Being male is a matter of birth, but being a man was a matter of choice."* Wow! I had never heard such powerful teachings. I was ready and accepted the challenge to become the man that God had called me to be.

CHAPTER 19

Free at Last, Free at Last!

"… Thank God almighty we are free at last."
– Dr. Martin Luther King, Jr.

The date was July 21st, 2003. It was finally here. Six and a half years had passed and now it was time to set my plans in motion. It was time to go home. What a glorious day that was. I remember being in prison and being inspired by Martin Luther King Jr, the life he led and what he stood for. How he fought for his people with peace and gave his life for what was right. I remember reading his "I have a dream" speech. I wanted to be a Martin Luther King Jr for my time.

My precious wife picked me up at the Walls Unit where I was released. What a glorious day, free at last, free at last, thank God Almighty I was free at last. But I was soon going to find out that freedom comes with a cost.

Most men that are released from prison have no idea what they are up against. Especially if they were incarcerated for multiple years, and/or had been to prison more than twice.

And I am talking about those who "want" to change their lives. They thought that just because they had great plans, good intentions and even gave their lives to God, everything would work out, that they would find a job and live happily ever after. Wrong!

So a special note to my ex-convict friends, and even if you're not an ex-convict. Maybe you've just had a bad life. You come from a broken family. You didn't have a father. You're struggling with drugs and alcohol. Whatever the case might be.

"**If**," and I repeat, "**If**" you really want to change your life. **If** you want a better life for yourself. Get ready to face some of the hardest and toughest challenges you will ever have to face. Emotional challenges, physical challenges, personal challenges, financial challenges and more.

But there is good news. In fact I would call it great news. And that is, that *change is possible!* And more than possible. And it can become a reality for you. That's the whole purpose of this book. To bring you the reality of what is really possible "If" you believe. If you choose to believe.

At the end of this book I will give you some concrete guidelines to get you started on the right road to successful living.

CHAPTER 20
The Untold Story

"I Never Thought it Would Happen to Me"

What I am about to tell you is not something I am proud of nor am I excited to share with you. But I believe I must share it because this happens to so many people. I never thought that it would happen to me, but it did.

Upon my release from prison I was ready. I had goals, I had dreams and I even had a written plan of action. I am talking about I had written what I was going to do from day one. My first week, my first month. I had my first six month goals and yearly goals. I even had a five, ten and twenty year plan. I mean I was ready. My plan was to get a job in some re-modeling or construction company, work for at least a year, just to get my feet on the ground, buy a few tools and start my own business in my second year out.

Things started great. I was on parole and was put on the ankle monitor. That didn't bother me because I knew it would only be for two or three months. I got a job my very first week out of prison. But then I lost my job a month later. They said I was too slow. They didn't quite put it in those words but I know that's what they meant. I remember calling my wife and telling her what had happened. So I decided to go ahead and start my own business. Remember, I had a plan. I had not been out a year yet but since I lost my job I just decided to put the plan into action.

It was eight a.m. Monday morning when I got fired. That very same day I did the following:

I got my first phone (A number I still have).

I put an ad in the newspaper.

I went and bought an answering machine (Yes they still sold answering machines). And…

I got my first job. All in one day.

"CQR Kitchen and Bath Remodeling Specialists" was born.

Things were great. I got off the ankle monitor. People started calling from the ad. I actually started getting more jobs, and I even bought an old truck from my Tio Jamin. My plans were coming to pass. Then my wife got pregnant. Wow, I am going to have a son. But then the unthinkable happened.

First I started smoking to relax. But then I drank my first beer and started going to dances with my sister. I didn't see anything wrong with smoking, dancing and having a beer once in a while. Yes, I was a Christian but I wasn't doing anything wrong. I was a hard worker with dreams and plans. But it was like my wife wanted to live in church. It seemed like all she thought of was church, church, church. And all I thought of was work, work, and work.

It wasn't like I was going to go back to drugs. I am not that stupid to go back to drugs. But the time and the place came when I took my first hit of cocaine, again. By the time my son was born on November 2nd, 2004, I was hooked on cocaine again. The unthinkable had happened. My wife was devastated and I couldn't believe what was happening to me. By December 2004 I was on a binge and gone for days.

January came around and on January 11th, 2005, I found myself at a motel smoking crack. I was at the end of my self-will. I couldn't believe what had happened to me. Was this it for me? Was I going back to prison? Was this really happening to me?

Thank God for my uncle Keno. He was the last person that I thought would come to my rescue. He heard what was happening to me and he came to pick me up and took me to a rehab center. That saved me, believe it or not. It's called the Mercy and Grace of God.

CHAPTER 21
My Next Life Mentor

"Dan the man with the master plan"

I was in the rehab hospital for five days. How in the world did this happen to me? I had goals, I had dreams, and I had plans. I wasn't sure why all this was happening to me. I prayed to God to help me understand what in the world was wrong with me. I begged God to please help me get back on track. And once again God showed Himself merciful and faithful.

A friend of mine once told me that everyone should have at least three kinds of coaches or mentors in their life: A financial coach, a life coach and a spiritual coach. Well, I was about to meet my next life mentor. Dan the man!!

In the rehab hospital they referred me to a few twelve step programs. I had been in rehabs before and I wasn't too crazy about going to some twelve step program. I figured I would just get more involved in my church. But at this point I was

95

willing to do anything to get back on track. I found myself in a place called "LA Vida Nueva Club." This is where I met Dan the man. La Vida Nueva Club was a CA program (Cocaine Anonymous). Very similar to the AA program. In fact they used the same AA book.

Dan became my sponsor, my mentor. Dan was a very interesting character to say the least. To be totally honest with you he seemed very weird to me at first. But there was something about him that caught my attention. He seemed very sincere and very smart. I'll never forget the questions he asked me when I accepted his offer to mentor me. Our conversation went something like this.

He said, "Do you really want to stay sober?"

I said yes.

He said, "Are you willing to go to any length to stay sober?"

I said yes.

Then he said. "Are you sure you want to stay sober and are willing to go to any length?"

With a little frustration I said, "YES!"

He said, "Ok, so if you want me to help you, here are my requirements. You must agree to do this:

1. I want you to read this every morning and this every night before you go to bed. (He handed me the AA book and showed me what I would be reading.)

2. You must call me every morning before nine a.m., after you have read your morning reading.

3. You "must" come to ninety meetings in ninety days. (There's that word "must" again.) In other words, every day.

At this point I stopped him and said, "Wait a minute. What do you mean every day?"

He said, "Every day. We have meetings every day and you need to come to every meeting for the next ninety days."

I said to him, "I don't mind coming to meetings but every day? Is that really necessary?"

But then Dan asked me, "Why is that such a problem? Did you use cocaine every day??" Wow!

He got me there. It made sense to me. Then he said, "Didn't you just tell me that you were willing to go to any length to stay sober?"

I wasn't sure how all this was going to work but I sure didn't want to go back to my old life and obviously there was something wrong with me. I at least knew that much. I decided to trust Dan. And I am so glad that I did. Dan was God sent. I truly believe that God put Dan in my path for the sole purpose of putting me back on track. It was like I was missing something in my thinking and my perspective in life and Dan would be the one to help me sort it out.

I did my ninety days and more. Dan became a great friend and mentor. For the next five years Dan worked with me and he taught me everything he knew about staying sober. He taught me that if I wanted to stay sober I would have to learn to work with other drug addicts. And this is where my burden for reaching out to men was rekindled. I had found my calling. It was like the missing link to my life. What Dan taught me was priceless and I will forever be grateful for what he did for me.

I never drank or touched drugs again. But the day came when I had to make a decision. Do I commit my life to the "program" or do I commit my life to my church? I came to the conclusion that my church wasn't as crazy as I thought they were. My church was in the business of disciplining men for the "harvest field" and that was exactly what I wanted to do, find men and challenge them. We need men!!

We desperately need men in our society today. We desperately need Godly fathers, Godly husbands and Godly leaders. I made my choice. But where do I start? I didn't necessarily want to be a pioneer. I just didn't believe that was where I belonged. I decided to just trust God. And I knew exactly where to start. The prayer room. "Everyday?" Hmmm.

CHAPTER 22

The Choose to Change Foundation Is Born A 501(C)3 Non-Profit

I knew God had saved me for a reason but I wasn't sure for what. I started coming to prayer at my church every morning. I started seeking God for direction. I wanted to help people change their lives, especially men, but how? God had put in my heart that we desperately needed men in our society, and I could see it so clearly. And what I mean by that is that we needed men who would be willing to stop living their selfish, self-centered lives and rise up and become the fathers, the husbands and the leaders that our society so desperately needs. We are living in a fatherless generation and there isn't enough said or taught about manhood, about men who love their children, love their wives and lead their families. I decided I was going to go find a few good men and challenge them. And I decided to start in the Texas prison system.

The *Choose to Change Foundation* was born, "believing in the impossible," with a mission of "restoring families by inspiring, challenging and equipping men to become more effective fathers, husbands and leaders in our community." We are on the front lines of fatherlessness, drug addiction and family violence.

I wanted to go into the prisons and parole offices as a motivational speaker, not a preacher. And the reason for that was simple. I knew what the Texas prisons were like. Everyone knows about Jesus in prison. What was missing was for men to be inspired, challenged and equipped. But not from just anyone, from one of their own. I thought that if these guys could hear and see one of their own, a loser father, a loser husband and a loser drug addict, become successful that they too would be able to believe for their own lives and families as well.

What I knew for a fact was that there were many men in the prison system that were just like me. They wanted to change their lives, they wanted a better future, and they didn't want to be losers anymore. But like me, they had ruined their lives and felt like "change" wasn't possible for them. My goal was to go find those men and challenge them to believe in the impossible, just like I had done.

I wasn't sure how all this would pan out, but again, God showed himself faithful.

I started going into our local parole office in McAllen, Texas, sharing my story with these men and inviting them to our church, and men started responding. God was moving and men started coming. Then I spoke to my Pastor, Roman Gutierrez, about starting some kind of class or program where I could invite these guys to come. And the Choose to Change Mentoring Program was born.

I started teaching men personal development and life skills. I started teaching them everything I had learned myself and the challenges I had to face getting out of prison. I started teaching them everything I knew about life change, personal development, personal responsibility, character building and more. All I wanted to do was give men a vision and a starting point to their better future.

At the same time I started going into the local prison and volunteering two hours a week there. I remember I would go every Thursday from five p.m. to six p.m. And then I would rush to church where I also had my mentoring class on Thursday from seven p.m. to eight p.m. I did this for two years or more.

Then one day I walked into my pastor's office and I walked out an evangelist. Wow!! A loser drug addict turns business man, turns entrepreneur, turns international evangelist. All because I chose to believe in the impossible.

Chapter 23
Final Thoughts

Today I travel the world sharing my story of hope and inspiration to whoever will hear it. I am a motivational speaker, a personal development teacher and a mentor to many. I go into schools, business organizations and churches. I speak in prisons, rehab centers and institutions.

As the CEO and Founder of the *Choose to Change Foundation*, I do personal development seminars, training and workshops. The *Choose to Change Foundation* has expression all over the world thanks to the many volunteers that believe in what we are doing and the fellowship of churches I am associated with. At the time of this writing, just in the State of Texas alone we go into the parole offices in McAllen, Harlingen, Laredo, Austin, San Antonio, El Paso and Victoria.

And I believe we are just getting started.

I live an amazing life. And I don't say all this to impress you, but to press upon you that God is still in the miracle working business. That if you would only choose to believe, all things are possible to him who believes. I heard a speaker once say, "If you choose to, you can change your life forever. If you choose to, you never have to be the same again."

CHAPTER 24

"But Do You Want to Change Your Life?"

If the answer to that question is "yes" then we can help you.

I hope my story has inspired you to believe for greatness in your life. The biggest challenge I see in our society today is that people cannot see their great need for God. More specifically, their need for Jesus Christ in their life. And if they do see it, they are confused about who to trust, who to turn to or where to go. And for good reason.

We live in such a "religious," reality show kind of world that people are just lost and confused. They have been hurt by preachers and churches. Televangelists have let them down. They don't know what to believe any more. And the reason I know this is because that's exactly what happened to me. But thank God I found truth in Jesus Christ.

So many people's lives are so twisted that they truly need a miracle in their lives. I came to the realization that there is only one miracle worker and His name is Jesus Christ. Now I know there are plenty of religions, churches and even a few magicians out there, but I am telling you there is only one miracle worker and His name is Jesus Christ. So if you are ready to change your life, the first step into the "process of change" is accepting Jesus Christ into your life. And I would count it a privilege if you allowed me to lead you in a short prayer of salvation.

Pray this prayer with me:

Lord Jesus, I thank you for your grace in my life. Today I make the decision to commit my life into your hands. I believe you died for me and that on the third day you rose again for the remission of my sins. Please forgive me of my sin and come into my heart. I pray you guide me and lead me in the right direction as I commit my life into your hands. In Jesus' name I pray. Amen.

Awesome!

Congratulations. Welcome to the family. So what now? Find a Bible preaching church. If you need help finding a church, especially in Texas, or anywhere in the world for that matter, contact us at the *Choose to Change Foundation* and we will help you find a church.

I am in the process of writing my next book and it will focus on the "process of change." So please watch out for it or go to my website and see if it is already out. Thanks for taking the time to read this book, God bless.

Four Powerful *Choose to Change* Testimonies

If these guys could do it, anyone can, if you choose to!

My name is Oscar Cruz from Brownsville, Texas. I had been involved in gangs, drugs and violence for years. My criminal life style started fast and at a very young age. By the age of fifteen I was already in TYC (The Texas Youth Commission). I was so bad that I was sentenced to a nine month term to TYC and wound up serving three years. In and out of TYC and finally, at eighteen years old, I graduated into the Texas adult prison system. After years of violence, drug addiction and gang life, I finally lost my family and found myself in prison (TDCJ, Texas Department of Criminal Justice) for the third time.

I wanted to change my life, but like many men in my situation, I didn't think it was possible. While in prison I decided to give God a try. I had prayed to God to please guide me in the right direction upon my release. I knew I couldn't make it on my own. The *Choose to Change Foundation* was there for me when I got out. When I heard Orlando at the parole office, I immediately knew God had heard my prayers. Hearing his story was like hearing my own. I started attending the **Choose to Change Mentoring Program** and I looked into the church that they were affiliated with. I felt the call to do something for God so I looked into the discipleship program that my church offered. God had heard my prayers.

Today my family has been restored and I am the senior pastor at a small community church. I am a father to my children, a husband to my wife and a leader in my family. I am so grateful for what God has done in my life. And I would like to give a special thank you to my Pastor, Roman Gutierrez, and *The Door Christian Fellowship* in McAllen, Texas. And of course to all the staff and volunteers at the *Choose to Change Foundation* for all their hard work. Please give to the *Choose to Change Foundation* today. They are doing amazing work at restoring family and fighting against fatherlessness, drug addiction and family violence.

My name is John Andrew Zapata. I grow up in a broken home and had a very rough childhood. Gangs, drugs and violence became a part of my life at a very early age and devastated my life and the life of my family. By the time I was seventeen I was on my way to prison. On my second trip to prison I had been arrested for homicide and four counts of aggravated kidnapping. They were offering me eighty years. I thought my life was over.

Then to top it off, my girlfriend, Sandra, came to see me. I was going to tell her to go her own way because I was going to prison for a long time. But everything changed when she told me she was pregnant. I couldn't believe it! I was going to have a son and now I wasn't going to be around to see him. I remember just breaking down and begging God to help me. I had never been religious and I didn't know how to pray. All I knew was that I wanted my son to have a father. I couldn't stand the thought of my own son having to go through what I had to go through. I never knew my father and it was a terrible feeling.

I didn't want to be a loser anymore. I wanted to be a father to my son. I made a decision that I wanted to change my life. So on my knees, in that prison cell, I gave my life to Jesus Christ. I started praying for a miracle and to my surprise the miracle came. I don't know how or why but the judge had grace on me. They dropped some charges and only gave me a three year sentence. I couldn't believe it! God had given me another chance at life and I took it.

Immediately I started learning, reading my Bible and getting involved in any Christian activity that was available to me in prison. One of the things I started praying for was direction and a mentor. Someone that could guide me in the right direction. That's when the *Choose to Change Foundation* came into our prison and I met Orlando. I knew it was an answered prayer. I remember that first day in class like it was yesterday. Orlando spoke with truth, power and authority. He knew what he was talking about. I remember him telling us that he had come looking for a few good men. He was holding nothing back.

He said he was there to challenge us to stop being losers and to rise up to become the men we were called to be. Men of God, fathers, husbands and leaders. I had never heard anyone speak like he did. It was like he was talking just to me. It was exactly what I was looking for. And I took his challenge.

I told Orlando that I wanted to be the man God had called me to be. He told me he would help me.

The day finally came. I got out of prison and started attending the **Choose to Change Mentoring Program.** It was amazing to see other men like me who had made a decision to change their lives and were making it in the free world as Christians. It really gave me hope that I too could succeed. I started attending church on a regular basis and started serving as an usher.

Today God has restored my family and given me a purpose in life. My girlfriend is now my wife. We now have two beautiful children and I am a father, a husband and a leader in my family. I am so grateful to Orlando and the *Choose to Change Foundation.* I decided to get involved in the discipleship program that the church offered and I am working to be a pastor one day. I would like to give a special thanks to my Pastor, Roman Gutierrez, for his leadership and for believing in me. And to the great brothers and sisters of my church, The Door Christian fellowship in McAllen, Texas.

My name is Daniel Martinez. I was raised in a family of seven, six brothers and one sister. My father was in and out of prison and a gang member. At a very young age I was introduced to drugs and the gang life. Even though in my heart and mind I never wanted to be like my father, it seemed like I was following the steps of my father without even realizing it. I was in and out of juvenile detention centers and by the age of nineteen I was sent to prison for the first time. I was only there for one year and got out on parole.

I was back for the second time after only being out of prison for three months. But this time for more serious charges. Prison didn't really bother me much because I had just accepted in my mind that this is how my life would be, gangs, drugs and prison. I put tattoos all over my head and body and my god was "la muerte."

Then one day in solitary confinement someone handed me a religious book. With nothing to do in solitary I decided to read this book. To my surprise the real God of heaven touched my heart and in that little solitary confinement cell I gave my life to Jesus Christ. I can't explain why or how it happened, all I know is that an overwhelming desire to change my life was born in me that day. There is much to say and many details to my story but to make a long story short, I made a decision that I was going to change my life. I sent word to my gang member friends that I was done and that I had given my life to God. I started praying for direction and asking God to help me find a church when I got out.

I met Orlando at the parole orientation when I got out of prison. I had accepted Jesus Christ in solitary confinement and I really wanted to change my life, but I wasn't sure if a man like me could change. But when I heard Orlando speak and what the Choose to Change organization did, I knew God had answered my prayers. I immediately started attending the Church and the Choose to Change Mentoring Program. I was amazed at the level of teaching that this class offered to anyone who was interested in changing their lives. I looked into the church and moved into the men's home. I got a job and started paying off all my court fees and fines that I owed and I finally got my driver's license. I joined the discipleship program and started serving in my church.

Today I am happily married to my beautiful and amazing wife (That is a miracle in itself), I am a bible study leader, an usher, a concert preacher and I am working toward being a pastor one day. It has been an amazing journey and I am so grateful to God and my Lord Jesus Christ for His Mercy and Grace. I want to thank my Pastor, Pastor Roman Gutierrez, for his leadership and all the brothers and sisters of the Door Christian Fellowship of McAllen, Texas.

My name is Rudy Cordova. All my life I had been a drug dealer, this is all I knew. I never had a legal job in my life. The third time to prison was the last straw for me. I had already lost my first marriage to the drug life and I wanted to change my life but I wasn't sure how to go about it. I didn't want anything to do with Jesus or going to church. But I was invited to a church service one day and I finally stopped fighting and gave my life to Jesus Christ. I got a job in a restaurant as a dish washer, a job I hated, but my life started to change.

Then one day I heard about the **Choose to Change Mentoring Program** and I decided to go and see what it was all about. Orlando's teachings on personal development, personal responsibility and character building literally changed my whole perspective on life. The Choose to Change Mentoring Program helped me develop a clearer direction for my life and gave me a starting point to a better and brighter future.

Today I own my own business and I am happily married to my beautiful wife, Jamie. We have two great sons, Christian and our newest addition to the family little Benjamin. I'm so grateful to God, to my Pastor, Roman Gutierrez, and the Choose to Change Mentoring Program for their commitment to restoring families just like mine.

ABOUT THE AUTHOR

Orlando Salinas is a motivational speaker, successful businessman, and the Founder and CEO of *Choose to Change Foundation*. To learn more about his programs, products and services or to have him speak at your next event, contact:

Choose to Change Foundation

2112 W. University Dr. #608

Edinburg, TX 78539

956-929-9560

www.Osalinas.com

www.ChooseToChangeFoundation.com

- Keynote speaker
- 1 and 2-day personal development seminars and workshops.
- *The Power of Choice*
- *Believing in the Impossible*
- *The Process of Change*

- *But Do You Want to Change Your Life* Seminar
- And more.

Made in the USA
Monee, IL
12 February 2020